the new york times

great
songs of
the sixties

volume 2

the new york times

great songs... of the sixties

volume 2

edited by milton okun

Quadrangle/The New York Times Book Co.

Distributed to the book trade by Harper & Row

Distributed to the music trade by Cherry Lane Music Co.

Library of Congress Catalog Card Number: 70-125482
International Standard Book Number: 0-8129-0479-6
Published by Quadrangle/The New York Times Book Co.
Distributed to the book trade by Harper & Row
Distributed to the music trade by Cherry Lane Music Co.
Printed in the United States of America

Music Engravings: Music Art Co.

Contents

Introduction

When Volume One of *The New York Times GREAT SONGS OF THE SIXTIES* was published, the decade loomed so large that possibly the view taken of the musical and social explosions was too close.

The violence and the tensions, the great changes that characterized the period, were reflected in a popular music that became a predominant international art form. With *SIXTIES 2* it is possible to look back on the sixties with more objectivity and see things in greater perspective.

It is gratifying to see that the choice of Bob Dylan, Paul Simon, Bacharach and David, and Lennon and McCartney as the creative leaders of the sixties has been proved correct. All of them have, while changing their directions in the seventies, kept their positions as innovators.

Many other leading talents of that time, Joni Mitchell, James Taylor, Kris Kristofferson, John Denver, Jimmy Webb, Neil Diamond, Gordon Lightfoot and others have grown and blossomed further in the seventies and have established themselves as major contributors.

What must now be accepted without serious questions is that popular songs in the sixties reached a new height of literacy, poetry, relevance and musical invention. It makes the job of an editor easy when doing a second volume. There is nothing in this collection that is second best. The standards for inclusion are the same. A song must be a fine composition. It cannot depend on the sound, production technique or instrumentation of a hit record and must be good when played on piano or guitar and sung by an untrained singer. Many of the creations of the new breed of writers of the sixties fit into this category. For example, some of the most heavily produced records of the Beatles, when translated down to piano and vocal arrangements, have the simple beauty of a Schubert lied.

The choice was made easier because a number of people gave me their opinions about songs which they felt should not have been left out of *SIXTIES 1*. That list alone gave me a head start towards the final compilation. Also, it is now apparent which songs have lasted, which are not dated, and which are being recorded and enjoyed today.

At a recent music conference in London, the president of one of the leading publishing companies was moaning for the good old times when not a day went by without some songwriter walking into his office with a new song, a beautiful new song. "Now you have to work so hard to find a beautiful song."

Years ago "all the beautiful new songs" came from a small group of men who worked in a twelve square block area in Manhattan known as Tin Pan Alley. Today, though songs don't knock on New York publishers' doors, they come from almost anywhere—a farm in the southwest, a Minnesota village, a Bronx tenement, a Quebec commune, an army camp in Texas—as wide a range as one could imagine.

One of the major developments in the sixties was the change from singers who sang material provided by paid songwriters to singers who wrote songs and performed them exactly as they felt they should be done, singers who wrote folk songs.

Now that we are midway into the seventies it is clear that the revolution brought about by a combination of the folk revival, the success of black music and the richness of the commitment of a young generation has taken hold. Our popular music today is not one dimensional, not restricted to a single kind of beat or lyric, or to one section of the country.

Playing these songs on the piano isn't just an exercise in nostalgia. It is a musical trip through new pathways of melody, rhythm and harmony. The richly textured music does not have to be associated with the period to be enjoyed and the advertising slogan used for *SIXTIES 1*—"a social document you can play on the piano"—seems an inadequate characterization. The music was less a social document than it was a creative tapestry of beauty and emotion. I believe that the multi-rhythmic laments of Lauro Nyro, the bi-tonal harmonies of Burt Bacharach, the children's songs of Tom Paxton, the brilliant alterations in traditional song forms such as Jim Webb's "MacArthur Park," the gemlike stories of Jerry Jeff Walker and Peter Yarrow will be affecting listeners and performers long after the tumult and trauma of the sixties are forgotten.

And When I Die

Words and Music by Laura Nyro

bun - dle up my cof - fin 'cause it's cold ____ way down there. I hear that it's
nev - er know by liv - in', only my dy - in' will tell. On - ly my
all I ask of dy - in' is to go ____ nat - 'ral - ly! On - ly wanna

cold way down there, yeah, ____ cra - zy cold a - way down
dy - in' will tell, yeah, ____ only my dy - in' will
go nat - 'ral - *(to Coda)*

there! ____
tell! ____
And when I die, and when I'm

gone, There'll be one child born and a world to car - ry

1. on, to car - ry on.

2. My on, to car - ry

on.

D.S. al Coda

gone, There'll be one child born and a world to car-ry

on. One child born when I die.

Repeat and fade

There'll be one child born when I die. There'll be

California Dreamin'

Words and Music by John Phillips

I passed a - long the way.   Oh, I got down on my

knees,   And I pre - tend to pray.

You know the preach-er likes the cold,   He knows I'm gon - na

stay.   Cal - i - for - nia dream - in'

(They Long To Be)
Close To You

Words by Hal David
Music by Burt Bacharach

an - gels got to - geth - er and de - cid - ed to cre - ate a dream come

true. So, they sprink - led moon dust in your hair of

gold and star - light in your eyes of blue. That is

Chelsea Morning

Words and Music by Joni Mitchell

Oh, won't you stay, we'll put on the day___ and we'll
Oh, won't you stay, we'll put on the day___ there's a
Oh, won't you stay, we'll put on the day___ and we'll

wear it till the night___ comes.___

sun show ev-'ry___ sec - ond.___
talk in pres - ent___ tens - es.

Now the cur - tain o - pens on a por - trait of to -
When the cur - tain clos - es and the rain - bow runs a -

by can-dle-light   by jew-el-light   if on - ly   you will ____

____   stay. _____   Pret - ty   ba - by, won't you

wake   up, ____   it's   a   Chel - sea ____   morn - ing. _____

A Day In The Life

Words and Music by John Lennon and Paul McCartney

Don't Think Twice, It's All Right

Words and Music by Bob Dylan

1. It ain't no use ___ to sit and won - der why, Babe ___
(2. It) ain't no use ___ in turn - in' on your light, Babe ___

It don't mat - ter an - y -
That light I nev - er

When the roost - er crows at the
Still I wish there was some - thin' you would

break of dawn
do or say

Look out your
To try and

win - dow and _____ I'll be gone.
make me change my _____ mind and stay.

You're the rea - son I'm trav - 'lin'
We nev - er did too _____ much talk - in' an - y -

ADDITIONAL VERSES

3. I'm walkin' down that long lonesome road, babe,
   Where I'm bound I can't tell.
   But goodbye's too good a word, gal,
   So I'll just say fare thee well.
   I ain't sayin' you treated me unkind,
   You could have done better but I don't mind.
   You just kind-a wasted my precious time,
   But don't think twice, it's all right.

4. It ain't no use in callin' out my name, gal,
   Like you never did before.
   It ain't no use in callin' out my name, gal,
   I can't hear you anymore.
   I'm a-thinkin' and a-wond'rin' all the way down the road,
   I once loved a woman, a child I'm told.
   I give her my heart but she wanted my soul,
   But don't think twice, it's all right.

Didn't We

Words and Music by Jimmy Webb

Very slowly

This time we al - most made the piec - es fit did - n't we girl? This time we al - most made some sense of it did - n't we girl? This time I had the an - swer

Follow Me

Words and Music by John Denver

*Guitarists: Tune lowest string to D.

up and down,____ all____ the way and all a - round,__

Take my hand__ and say you'll fol - low me.__

It's long been on my mind,__
You see, I'd like to share my life____

The 59th Street Bridge Song (Feelin' Groovy)

Words and Music by Paul Simon

Slow down,___ you move too fast.___ You got to make the morn-

read-y to sleep. Let the morn-ing-time drop all its pet-als on me.

Life, I love you, All is groov - y. _____

Repeat and fade out

Fire And Rain

Words and Music by James Taylor

Verses 1 & 2:

Just yes-ter-day morn-ing they let me know___ you were gone___
Look down up-on me, Je-sus, you've got to help me make a stand___

Su - san, the plans they made put an end to you.
You've just got to see me through an - oth - er day.

I walked out this morn - ing and I wrote down this song, ___
My bod - y's ach - ing and my time is at hand, ___

I just can't re - mem - ber who to send ___ it to. ___
And I ___ won't make it an - y oth - er way. ___

Chorus:

I've seen fire and I seen rain,   I've seen

49

sun - ny days_ that I thought would nev - er end,___ I've seen

lone - ly times_ when I could not find a friend,___ But I

al - ways thought that I'd see you a - gain.___

1. 2.
C9

2nd time to Verse 3

Fine
C9

2. Won't you
3. Now I'm

Fine

50

Verse 3:

walk-ing my mind to an eas-y time my back turned towards the sun.___

Lord knows when the cold wind blows it - 'll turn your head___ a - round,___ Well, there's

hours of time___ on the tel - e-phone line___ to talk a-bout things to come,___

D.S. al Fine

Sweet dreams and fly - ing ma - chines in pie - ces on _____ the ground.

51

Five Hundred Miles Away From Home

Words and Music by Bobby Bare, Charlie Williams, and Hedy West

miss you, son,___ we love you; Come on home."

___ Well, I

did - n't have to pack ___ I had it

all right on my back, Now I'm five hun - dred

miles ___ a - way from home. ___

Chorus:

A - way from home, a - way from home, Cold and

tired and all a - lone, Yes, I'm

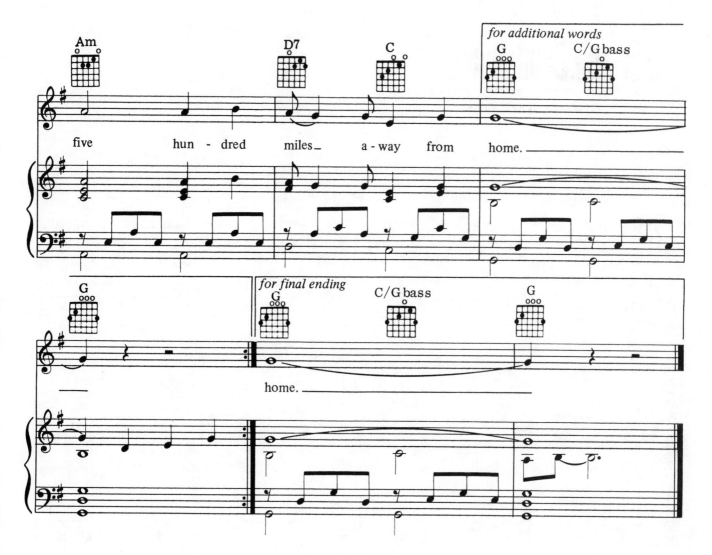

ADDITIONAL VERSES

2. *(Recitation over music)*
   I know this is the same road I took the day I left home,
   But it sure looks different now.
   I guess I look different, too,
   'Cause time changes everything.
   I wonder what they'll say
   When they see their boy lookin' this way?
   (Sung) I wonder what they'll say when I get home.

3. Can't remember when I ate,
   It's just thumb, walk and wait,
   And I'm still five hundred miles away from home.
   If my luck had been just right
   I'd be with them all tonight,
   But I'm still five hundred miles away from home.
   Chorus:
   Away from home, away from home,
   Cold and tired and all alone,
   Yes, I'm still five hundred miles away from home.
   Oh, I'm still five hundred miles away from home.

For The Good Times

Words and Music by Kris Kristofferson

For What It's Worth

Words and Music by Stephen Stills

1. There's bat - tle lines be - in' drawn, No - bod - y's
2. What a field day for the heat. A
3. Pa - ra - noi - a strikes deep,

right if ev - 'ry - bod - y's wrong,
thou - sand peo - ple in the street sing - in'
in - to your life it will creep. It

Young peo - ple speak - in' their minds, _____ Get - tin'
songs and car - ry - in' signs. _____ Most - ly
starts when you're al - ways a - fraid. _____ Step out of

To Coda

so much re - sis - tance from be - hind. I think it's time we
say - ing, "Hoo - ray for our side." _____
line the men come _____ and

stop, chil - dren, what's that sound? _ Ev - 'ry - bod - y look what's go - in' down. _____

take you a - way.____ You bet - ter

After repeat
D.S. al Coda

Coda

stop, hey, what's that sound?___ Ev -'ry-bod - y look what's go - in' down. You bet - ter

Repeat and fade

Give Peace A Chance

Words and Music by John Lennon and Paul McCartney

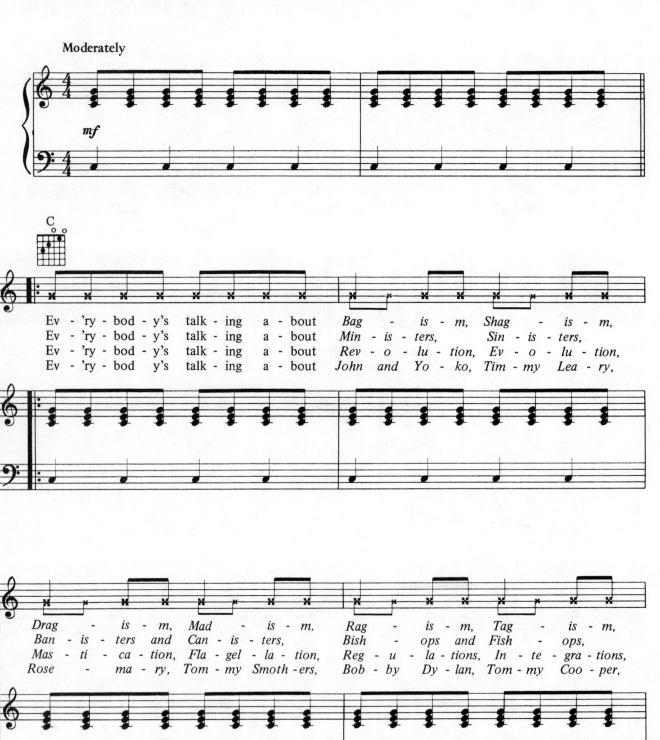

This is - m, That is - m, Is - n't it the most?
Rab - bits and Pop - eyes, Bye - bye Bye - byes.
Med - i - ta - tion, U-nit-ed Na - tions, Con - grat - u - la - tions.
De - rek Tay - lor, Nor - man Mail - er, Al - an Gins - berg, Ha - re Krish - na

Ha - re, Ha - re Krish-na.

All we are say -

ing is give peace a

chance.

Grazing In The Grass

Words by Harry Elston
Music by Philemon Hou

trip! Just watch-ing as the world goes by. *Graz-ing in the grass is a gas,*

ba - by, can you dig it? There are so man - y groov - y things to

see while graz - ing in the grass. *Graz-ing in the grass is a gas,*

So real, — so real, — so real, — so real, — so real. — Can you
Can you

dig it?
dig it?

I can dig it, he can dig it, she can dig it, we can dig it,

Repeat ad lib and fade out

they can dig it, you can dig it.   Oh,   let's dig it!   *Can you dig — it,   ba - by?*

Guantanamera

Words by Jose Marti
Music adaptation by Hector Angulo and Pete Seeger

mo - rir - me quie - ro   E - char mis   ver - sos del   al - ma.

2. Mi verso es de un verde claro
   Y de un carmin encendido
   Mi verso es de un verde claro
   Y de un carmin encendido
   Mi verso es un cierro herido
   Que busca en el monte amparo.
   (Chorus)

3. Con los pobres de la tierra
   Quiero yo mi suerte echar
   Con los pobres de la tierra
   Quiero yo mi suerte echar
   El arroyo de la sierra
   Me complace mas que el mar.
   (Chorus)

(Literal English Translation)

1. I am a truthful man, from the
   land of palm trees. Before
   dying, I want to share these
   poems of my soul.

2. My poems are light green,
   but they are also flaming
   crimson. My verses are like
   a wounded faun, seeking
   refuge in the forest.

3. With the poor people of this
   earth, I want to share my fate.
   The little streams of the
   mountains please me more
   than the sea.

He Ain't Heavy...He's My Brother

Words by Bob Russell
Music by Bobby Scott

broth-er. _____ So on we go;

his wel - fare is my con - cern. _____ No bur - den is

he to bear, _____ we'll get _____ there. _____

And the load _____ does-n't weigh me

down at all; _____ He ain't heav-y, _____

he's my broth-er. _____

rit.

Here Comes The Sun

Words and Music by George Harrison

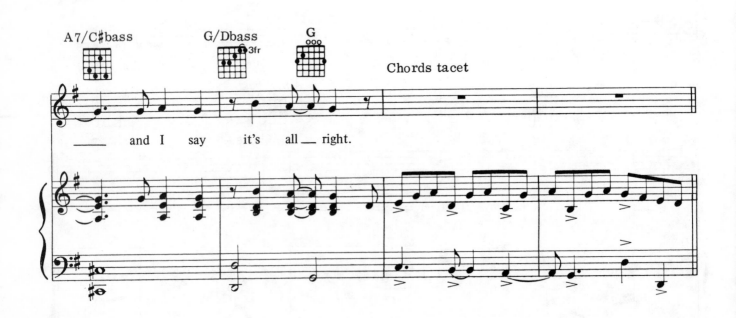

Lit - tle dar -ling, it's been_ a long_ cold lone - ly win -
Lit - tle dar -ling, the smiles_ re - turn - ing to_ their fac -

ter.
es.
Lit - tle dar -ling, it feels_ like years_
Lit - tle dar -ling, it seems_ like years_

__ since it's_ been here._
__ since it's_ been here._
Here comes_ the sun,_

___ here comes_ the sun,_ (And I say)

it's all __ right.

Sun,

In this - and all - meter changes in this song, the 8th note remains the same.

here comes— the   sun—

it's   all—right!

It's   all—right!

Honey

Words and Music by Bobby Russell

See the tree, how big it's grown, But friend it has-n't been too long, it

Then the first snow came and she ran out to brush the snow a-way so it

was-n't big

would-n't die

I laughed at her and she got mad, the

Came run-nin' in all ex-cit-ed

miss you _____ and I'm be - ing good _____

And I'd love to be with you _____ If on - ly I could.

She could.

One

day while I was not at home, While she was there and all a - lone the

an - gels came   Now all I have are mem - o - ries of

Hon - ey and I wake up nights and call her name.   And

now my life's an emp - ty stage Where Hon - ey lived and Hon - ey played and

love grew up   A small cloud pass - es o - ver - head and

cries down on the flow - er bed that Hon - ey loved. _____

Holly Holy

Words and Music by Neil Diamond

96

ly sun

Hol - ly ho - ly rain.

Hol - ly ho - ly

love.

I Am A Rock

Words and Music by Paul Simon

Slowly

1. A win-ter's day ___ In a deep and dark De-
walls, ___ A for - tress deep and
love; ___ I've heard the word be -
books ___ And my po - et - ry to pro -

land.

2. I've built
3. Don't talk of
4. I have my land._____ And a rock can feel no

pain; And an is-land nev - er cries._____

From the Rock Opera "Jesus Christ Superstar"

I Don't Know How To Love Him

Words by Tim Rice
Music by Andrew Lloyd Webber

ver - y man - y ways   He's just one more

Should I bring him down ___ should I scream and shout ___

___ Should I speak of love ___ let my feel-ings out? ___ I nev-er thought I'd

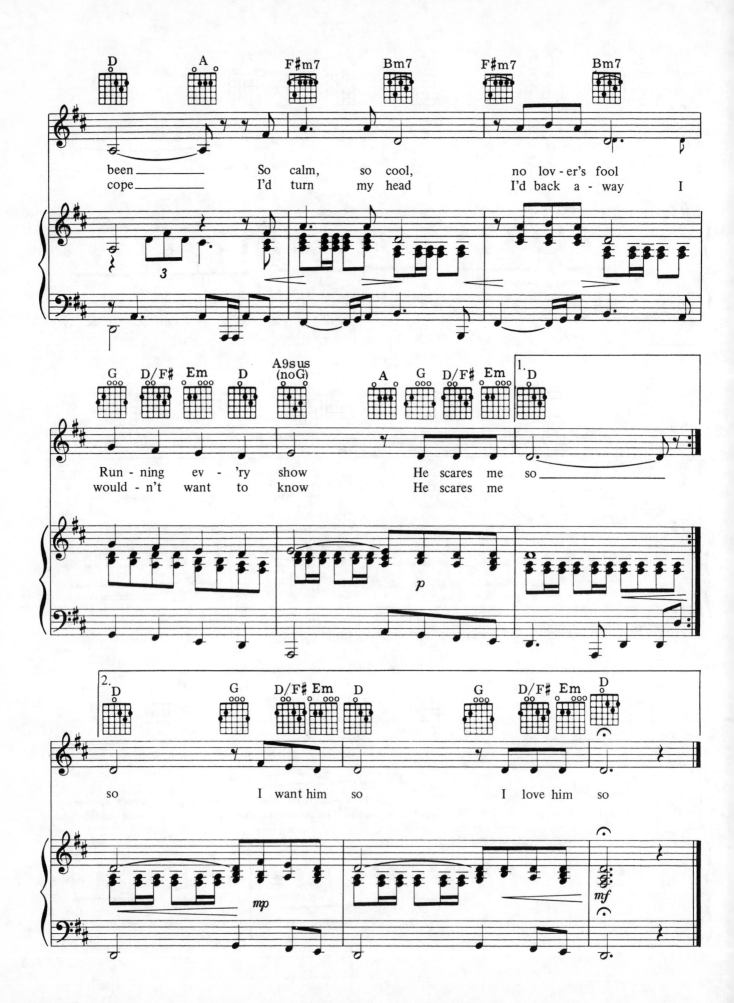

I Shall Be Released

Words and Music by Bob Dylan

They say ev-'ry-thing can be re-placed, _____
They say ev-'ry man _____ needs pro-tec-tion, _____

yet ev-'ry dis-tance is not near. _____ So I re-mem-ber ev-'ry
they say ev-'ry man must _____ fall. _____ Yet I swear I see my re-

face ___ of ev-'ry man who put me here. ___
flec-tion ___ some place so high a-bove this wall. ___

(falsetto harmony)

I see my light come shin-in' ___ from the West un-to the East. ___

An-y day ___ now, ___ an-y day ___ now, ___

I shall be re-leased.

To Coda

110

Stand-ing next to me in this lone-ly crowd _____

is a man who swears he's not to blame._ All day long I hear his voice shout-in'

D.S. al Coda 𝄋

out so loud, cry-ing out that he was framed. _____

Coda

leased.

If You Could Read My Mind

Words and Music by Gordon Lightfoot

Play thumb and finger style. Medium Latin feeling as in a beguine. G.L.

feet. But sto-ries al-ways end, and if you read be-tween the lines, you'd know that I'm just tryin' to un-der-stand the feel-in's that you lack. I nev-er thought_ I could

feel this way— and I've got to say— that I just don't get it. I don't know where

we went wrong,—but the feel-in's gone— and I just can't get it back!—

It's Not Unusual

Words and Music by Gordon Mills and Les Reed

Why can't this cra - zy love be mine?_____

It's not un - u - su - al___ to be mad with an - y - one.___

It's not un - u - su - al___ to be

Main Theme from the 20th Century-Fox Film
"The Prime of Miss Jean Brodie"

Jean

Words and Music by Rod McKuen

Moderately

Jean, Jean, ros - es are red,

all the leaves have gone green; _____ and the

I'll still be wait-in'. Jean, Jean, the ros - es are

red, all the leaves have gone green. ____ And the

hills are a - blaze with the moon's yel-low haze; come in - to my

arms, bon-nie Jean. Till the Jean. ____

Just Like A Woman

Words and Music by Bob Dylan

takes   just   like   a   wom - an,   Yes, she does, ___ She
fake   just   like   a   wom - an,   Yes, you do, ___ You

makes   love   just   like   a   wom - an,   Yes, she does, ___ And she
make   love   just   like   a   wom - an,   Yes, you do, ___ Then you

aches   just   like   a   wom - an, _____   But she breaks just like a lit - tle
ache   just   like   a   wom - an, _____   But you break just like a lit - tle

Lay, Lady, Lay

Words and Music by Bob Dylan

Un - til the break of _____ day,

let me see you make him smile. _

His clothes are dirt - y but his, his hands are clean; _

And you're the best _ thing that he's ev - er seen. _

morn-ing light,— I long to reach for you in the night.—

Stay, la - dy, stay,— stay while the night— is still a -

head.

Little Green Apples

Words and Music by Bobby Russell

And she reach - es out an' takes my hand, squeez - es it, says, "How you feel - in'

Hon."   And I look a - cross   at smil - ing lips that

warm my heart and see my morn - ing   sun.   And if that's not

it don't rain in In-di-an-ap-o-lis in the sum-mer time.___ And

when my-self is feel-in' low I think a-bout her face a-glow to ease my mind.

Some -

times I call her up at home know-ing she's bus-y___

And ask if she could get a-way and meet me_____ and grab a

bite to eat

And she drops what she's do-in' and

hur-ries down to meet me and I'm al-ways late.

But

she sits wait-ing pa-tient-ly and smiles when she first sees me 'cause she's made that way.

D.S. al Coda 𝄋

The Marvelous Toy

Words and Music by Tom Paxton

Moderate tempo

When I was just a wee lit-tle lad full of health and
(The) first time that I picked it up I had a big sur-
(It) first marched left and then marched right and then marched un-der a
(Well the) years have gone by too quick-ly it seems and I have my own lit-tle

joy, My fa-ther home-ward came one night, and
prise, For right on its bot-tom were two big but-tons and that
chair, And when I looked where it had gone, it
boy, And yes-ter-day I gave to him my

It   went "Zip" when it moved, And "Bop" when it stopped, And
It   still goes "Zip" when it moves, And "Bop" when it stops, And

"Whirr" when it stood still, I nev - er knew just
"Whirr" when it stands still, I nev - er knew just

what it was and I guess I nev - er will. The
what it was and I guess I nev - er will. It
Well the

will.

MacArthur Park

Words and Music by Jimmy Webb

Moderately

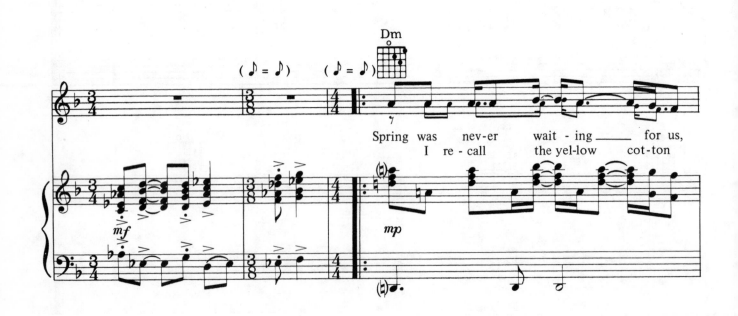

Spring was nev-er wait-ing ____ for us,
I re-call the yel-low cot-ton

Gm   Bb/F

pants.
trees.

Ab   Bb   C

Mac - Ar -thur's Park is   melt - ing   in   the dark,__

_mf_

Cmaj7   Gm7/C

__   all   the sweet green ic - ing flow - ing down.__

F   Fmaj7

Some - one left   the cake__ out__ in the rain;__   I   don't__

think that I___ can take it 'cause it took so long to bake___ it and I'll

nev-er have___ that rec-i-pe___ a-gain,   oh,

no.___

There will be an-oth-er song for me   for I will sing_____ it,___

there will be an-oth-er dream for me,   some-one will

bring_____ it.____ I will drink the wine_while it is warm_____

____ and nev-er let_you catch_me look-ing at the sun,_ and

af-ter all the loves_ of my life, af-ter all the loves_ of my

life_____ you'll_ still be the one. I will

154

Me And Bobby McGee

Words and Music by Kris Kristofferson and Fred Foster

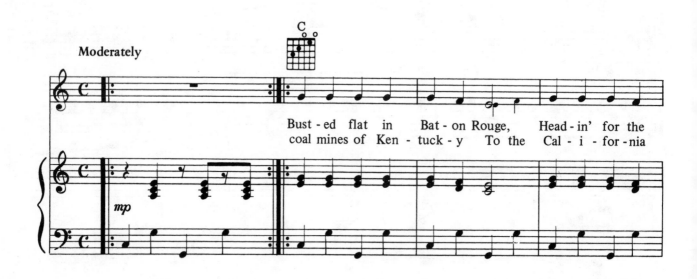

Bust-ed flat in Bat-on Rouge, Head-in' for the
coal mines of Ken - tuck - y To the Cal - i - for - nia

trains; Feel - in' near - ly fad - ed as my jeans, _____
sun, Bob - by shared the se - crets of my soul; _____

blues; _____ With them wind-shield wi-pers slap-pin' time and Bob-by clap-pin'
find; _____ And I'd trade all of my to-mor-rows for a sin-gle yes-ter-

hands We fin-'ly sang up ev-'ry song that driv-er knew.
day, Hold-in' Bob-by's bod-y next to mine.

Free-dom's just an - oth - er word for noth - in' left to lose,
Free-dom's just an - oth - er word for noth - in' left to lose,

Michelle

Words and Music by John Lennon and Paul McCartney

you'll un - der - stand.
know what I mean: I love you.

I want you, I want you, I want you, I think you know by

164

now,   I'll get to you some - how. ___ Un - til I do, I'm

tell - ing you, so you'll un - der - stand: Mi - chelle,

ma belle,   sont les mots qui vont tres bien en - semble, tres bien en -

semble. I will say the on-ly words I know that you'll un-der-

stand, my Mi-chelle.

Repeat and fade

Mr. Bojangles

Words and Music by Jerry Jeff Walker

ged shirt and bag - gy pants,_____ the
the eyes of age_____ as he

old soft shoe._____ He jumped so
spoke right out._____ He talked of

high, jumped so high,_____ Then he
life, talked of life,_____ he

light - ly touched down._____
laughed slapped his leg a step._____

3. He said his name, Bojangles,
Then he danced a lick across the cell.
He grabbed his pants a better stance
Oh, he jumped up high,
He clicked his heels.
He let go a laugh, let go a laugh,
Shook back his clothes all around. (Chorus)

4. He danced for those at minstrel shows and county fairs
Throughout the South.
He spoke with tears of fifteen years
How his dog and he
Traveled about.
His dog up and died, he up and died,
After twenty years he still grieved. (Chorus)

5. He said, "I dance now at ev'ry chance in honky tonks
For drinks and tips.
But most of the time I spend behind these county bars,"
He said, "I drinks a bit."
He shook his head and as he shook his head,
I heard someone ask please, (Chorus)

Music To Watch Girls By

Words by Tony Velona
Music by Sid Ramin

vene, To make the scene.___ Which is the name of the game, Watch a

guy watch a dame, On an - y street in town.___

Up and down,___ And o - ver and a - cross, Ro - mance is boss.___

Guys talk girl - talk

It hap -pens ev -'ry - where. Eyes watch

girls walk with ten - der lov - ing care.___ It's keep-ing

My Ramblin' Boy

Words and Music by Tom Paxton

He was a man ___ and a friend al - ways ___ He stuck with
In Tul - sa town ___ we chanced to stray ___ We thought we'd

me _____ in the hard old days _____ He nev-er cared _____ if I had no
try _____ to work one day _____ The boss said he _____ had room for

dough _____ We ram-bled 'round _____ in the rain and snow. _____ } And here's to
one _____ Says my old pal, _____ "We'd rath-er bum!" _____ }

Chorus:

you, _____ my ram-blin' boy, _____ May all your ram - blin' bring you

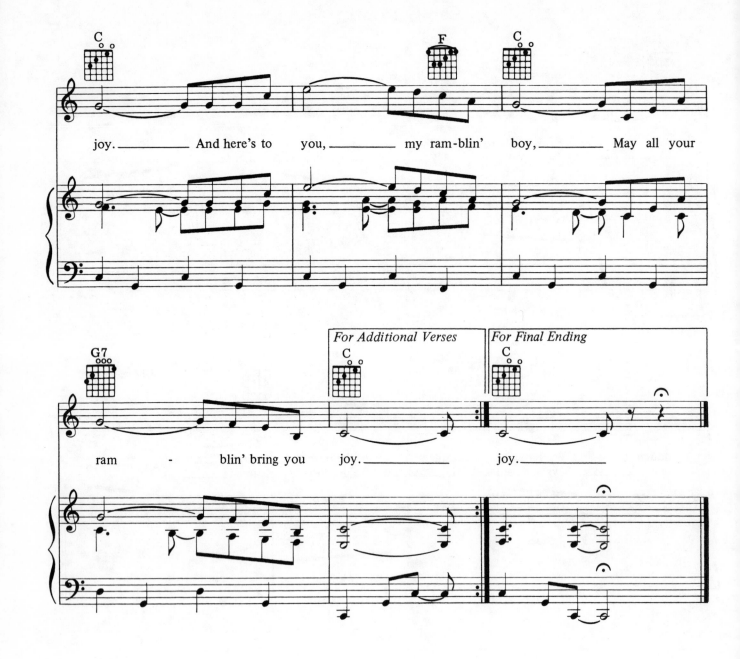

joy. _____ And here's to you, _____ my ram-blin' boy, _____ May all your

For Additional Verses

For Final Ending

ram - blin' bring you joy. _____ joy. _____

ADDITIONAL VERSES

3. Late one night in a jungle camp
   The weather it was cold and damp
   He got the chills and he got 'em bad
   They took the only friend I had.
   (Chorus)

4. He left me there to ramble on
   My ramblin' pal is dead and gone
   If when we die we go somewhere
   I'll bet you a dollar he's ramblin' there.
   (Chorus to final ending)

My Sweet Lady

Words and Music by John Denver

Dmaj7   Em/Dbass   D   Dmaj7   G/Dbass   Gm/Dbass

La - dy,__ you've been dream-ing__ I'm as close as I can__ be   and I
La - dy,__ my sweet la - dy__ I just can't be-lieve it's__ true   and it's
La - dy,__ my sweet la - dy__ I'm as close as I can__ be   and I

Last time to Coda ⊕

Dmaj7   Em   A   D   D7

swear   to you__   our   time   has just   be - gun.
like   I've nev - er   ev - er loved   be - fore.
swear   to you__   our   time   has just   be - *(To Coda)*

G   A   D   D7

Close   your eyes _____ and rest   your wear - y   mind   I

prom-ise I will stay right here be - side you

To -

day our lives were joined, be-came en - twined

I

wish that you could know how much I love

After Repeat,
D.S. 𝄋 al ⊕ Coda

you.

Coda ⊕

gun.

The Night They Drove Old Dixie Down

Words and Music by J. Robbie Robertson

In the win-ter of six-ty five, we were hun-gry, just bare-ly a-live.___ By May the tenth, Rich-mond had fell;___ it's a time___ I re-mem-ber, oh,___ so well.___ The

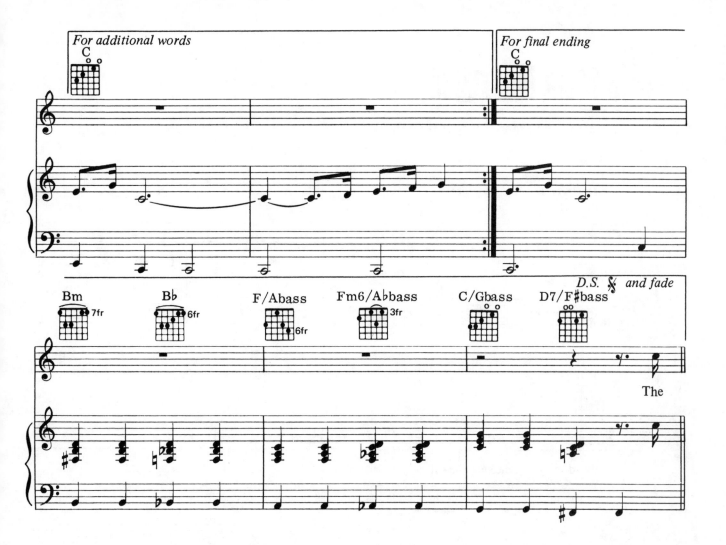

ADDITIONAL WORDS

Back with my wife in Tennessee
When one day she called to me
"Virgil, quick, come see:
There goes Robert E. Lee!"
Now, I don't mind choppin' wood
And I don't care if the money's no good,
Ya take what ya need and ya leave the rest
But they should never have taken
The very best.
(Repeat Chorus)

Like my father before me
I will work the land.
And like my brother above me
Who took a rebel stand.
He was just eighteen, proud and brave,
But a Yankee laid him in his grave.
I swear by the mud below my feet,
You can't raise a Caine back up
When he's in defeat.
(Repeat Chorus with final ending)

Okie From Muskogee

Words and Music by Merle Haggard and Roy Edward Burris

Moderately

Verse:

Eb

1. We don't smoke ma-ri - jua-na in Mus - ko-gee,_____
2. We don't make a par-ty out of lov - ing,_____
   boots are still in style if a man needs foot-wear,_____

And we don't take our trips on L. S.
But we like hold-ing hands and pitch-ing
Beads and Ro-man san - dals won't be

Bb7

D.
woo.
seen.

And we don't burn our draft cards down on
We don't let our hair grow long and
Foot-ball's still the rough-est thing on

Main Street,
shag - gy
cam - pus,

But we like liv - ing right and be - ing
Like the hip - pies out in San Fran - cis - co
And the kids here still re - spect the Col - lege

Eb

Chorus:

Eb

free.
do.
Dean.

And I'm proud to be an O - kie from Mus -

ko - gee;   A place where e - ven   squares can have a   ball.___

Bb7

We still wave Ol'   Glo - ry down at the

Court House,   White   light - ning's   still   the

Eb

1.2.   3.

big - gest   thrill of all._____   3. Leath - er ___

On The Way Home

Words and Music by Neil Young

Piece Of My Heart

Words and Music by Bert Berns and Jerry Ragavoy

Slowly, with a beat

Did-n't I make you feel like you were the on-ly man,—

Did-n't I give you ev-'ry-thing that a wom-an pos-si-bly can,—

But with all the love I give you, it's nev-er e-nough,— But

I'm gon-na show you, ba-by, that a wom-an can be tough.— So

go on, go on, go on, go on,

poco a poco cresc.

Take it! Take an-oth-er lit-tle piece of my heart now, ba-by,—

f

191

Break it! Break an-oth-er lit-tle piece of my heart now, hon-ey,___

Have a! Have an-oth-er lit-tle piece of my heart now, ba-by,___

You know you got it if it makes you feel good.___ *Fine*

You're out in the street look-in' good,___ And you know deep down

193

Puff, The Magic Dragon

Words and Music by Peter Yarrow and Leonard Lipton

Puff, the mag-ic drag - on lived by the sea and

frol - icked in the au - tumn mist in a land called Ho - nah - Lee,

Lit - tle Jack - ie Pa — per loved that ras - cal, Puff, and

brought him strings and seal - ing wax and oth - er fan - cy stuff, Oh!

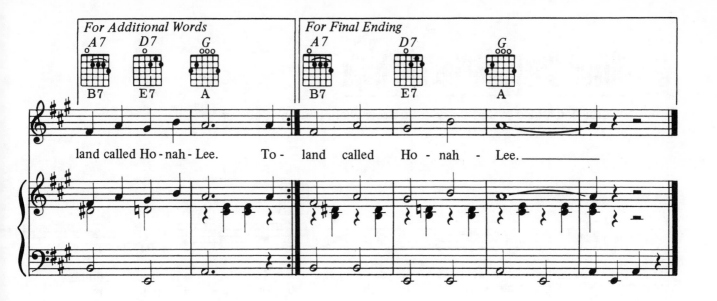

land called Ho - nah - Lee. To - land called Ho - nah - Lee._____

ADDITIONAL WORDS

2.   Together they would travel on a boat with billowed sail,
Jackie kept a lookout perched on Puff's gigantic tail,
Noble kings and princes would bow whene'er they came,
Pirate ships would low'r their flag when Puff roared out his name. Oh!
(Chorus)

3.   A dragon lives forever but not so little boys,
Painted wings and giant rings make way for other toys.
One grey night it happened, Jackie Paper came no more
And Puff that mighty dragon, he ceased his fearless roar. Oh!
(Chorus)

4.   His head was bent in sorrow, green scales fell like rain,
Puff no longer went to play along the cherry lane.
Without his life-long friend, Puff could not be brave
So Puff that mighty dragon, sadly slipped into his cave. Oh!
(Chorus)

River Deep, Mountain High

Words and Music by Jeff Barry, Ellie Greenwich, and Phil Spector

1. When I was a lit-tle girl,___ I had a rag doll,___
2. When you were a young boy did you have a pup-py___

the on-ly doll I've ev-er owned.___
that al-ways fol-lowed you a - round?___

Now I love you just the way___ I loved that rag doll,___
Well I'm gon-na be as faith-ful as that pup-py,___

but on-ly now my love has grown.__ And it gets
no, I'll nev-er let you down.__ 'Cause it goes

strong-er in ev-'ry way,__ and it gets
on and on__ like a riv-er flows,__ And it gets

deep-er, let me say,__ And it gets
big-ger, ba-by, and heav-en knows__ That it gets

high-er day by day.__ }
sweet-er, ba-by, as it grows.__ } And

do I love you, my oh my? _____ Yeah,

riv - er deep moun - tain high, __ yeah, yeah, yeah. __ And

if I lost you, would I cry? _____ Oh how I love you,

ba - by, ba - by, ba - by, ba - by. _____

To Coda ⊕   *D.C. al Coda*   ⊕ *Coda*

Sally, Go Round The Roses

Words and Music by Zel Sanders and Lona Stevens

1. Sal - ly, go 'round the ros - es. Sal - ly, go 'round the
2. Sal - ly, go 'round the ros - es. Sal - ly, go 'round the

ros - es. Sal - ly, go 'round the ros - es. Sal - ly, go 'round the
ros - es. Sal - ly, go 'round the ros - es. Sal - ly, go 'round the

pret - ty ros - es. The ros - es, they can't hurt you. No, the
pret - ty ros - es. They won't tell your se - crets.

ros - es, they can't hurt you. The ros - es, they can't
They won't tell your se - crets. They won't tell your

hurt you. No, the ros - es, they can't hurt you.
se - crets. No, the ros - es won't tell your se - crets.

Sal - ly, don't-cha go, don't-cha go down - town. Sal - ly, don't-cha
Sal - ly, ba - by, cry, let your hair hang down. Sal - ly, ba - by,

mf - f

Stoned Soul Picnic

Words and Music by Laura Nyro

Something

Words and Music by George Harrison

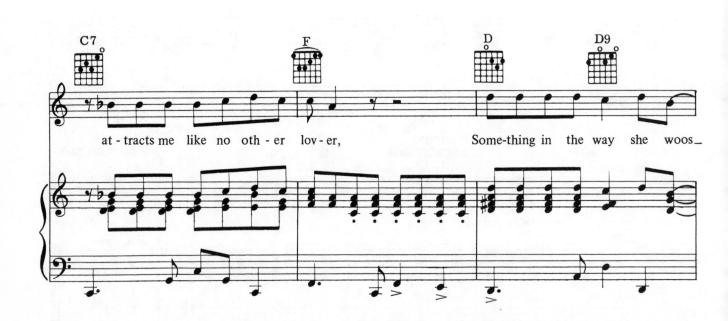

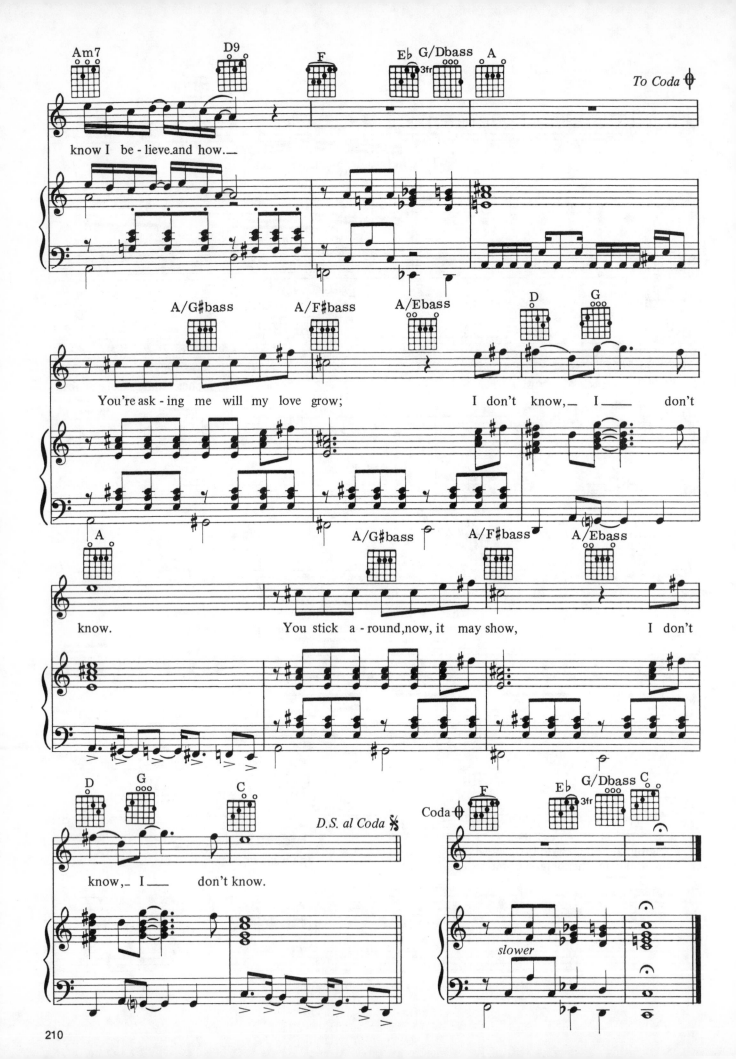

Sunshine Superman

Words and Music by Donovan Leitch

Sun - shine___ came soft - ly through my (a)-win-dow to - day,___
Ev' - ry-bod-y's hust - lin' just to have a lit - tle___ scene___

I'll pick up your hand and slow-ly blow your lit-tle mind,___ When you've made your mind up for-ev-er to be mine.___

Repeat and fade

Sugar, Sugar

Words and Music by Jeff Barry and Andy Kim

Hon-ey, ah,— Sug-ar, Sug-ar, You are my

can - dy girl — And you've got me want-ing you. —

I just can't be - lieve the love - li - ness of lov - ing you.
When I kissed you, girl, I knew — how sweet a kiss could be. (I

Sweet Baby James

Words and Music by James Taylor

works in the sad - dle and he sleeps in the can - yons   Wait - ing for
Berk - shires seemed dream - like on ac - count of that frost - ing, With ten miles be -

sum - mer his pas - tures to change. _____
hind me and ten thou - sand more to go. _____

And as the moon ris - es he
There's a song that they sing when they

Chorus:

Good - night, you moon - light lad - ies,____ Rock - a - bye,

sweet Ba - by James. Deep greens and blues are the

col - ors I choose, Won't you let me go down in my dreams,

And rock - a - bye, sweet Ba - by James. Now the

Sweet Blindness

Words and Music by Laura Nyro

been drink-in', Ain't gon-na tell you what I've been drink-in'; Wine of

won-der; won-der. By the way sweet blind-ness.

Now, ain't that sweet-eye blind-ness good to me.

Sweet Caroline

Words and Music by Neil Diamond

gin   to   know - in',   but   then   I   know   it's   grow - in'

strong.   Was   in   the   spring, ‿

then   spring   be - came   the   sum - mer ___   who'd - a   be -

From the Rock Opera "Jesus Christ Superstar"

Superstar

Words by Tim Rice
Music by Andrew Lloyd Webber

Ev - 'ry time I look at you I don't un - der stand____
Tell me what you think a - bout your friends at the top.____

Why you let the things you did get so out of hand;____
Who d'you think be - sides your - self's the pick of the crop?____

These Boots Are Made For Walkin'

Words and Music by Lee Hazlewood

fess.
bet.
burned.

You been mess - in' ___
You keep "same - in'" ___
I just found me a

where you should - n't been mess - in',
when you ought - a be chang - in',
brand - new box ___ of match - es,

And now
Now what's
___ And

some - one else ___ is get - tin' all ___ your best.
right is right, ___ but you ain't been ___ right yet.
what { he / she } knows, ___ you ain't got time ___ to learn.

This Guy's In Love With You

Words by Hal David
Music by Burt Bacharach

Until It's Time For You To Go

Words and Music by Buffy Sainte-Marie

now._____ This love of mine had no be - gin-ning, it has no

end,_____ I was an oak, now I'm a wil-low; now I can

bend._____ And though I'll nev-er in my life see you a -

me, _____ don't ask _____ for - ev - er of _ me,

cresc. poco a poco

love me, _____ love me, _____ now. _____ You're not a

dream, you're not an an - gel, you're a man, _____ I'm not a

dim. poco a poco

Watermelon Man

Words by Gloria Lynne
Music by Herbie Hancock

Coda

I will buy one from you ev-'ry day,___ Just be sure you'll

al-ways come my way,___ That would real-ly be wa-ter-mel-on.___

Wedding Bell Blues

Words and Music by Laura Nyro

Wichita Lineman

Words and Music by Jimmy Webb

Moderately

mf

B♭maj7   F6(9)

I am a line-man for the coun-ty,___   And I drive the main

Gm7   Dm   Am   G

road   Search-in' in the sun for an-oth-er___ o-ver load.___

And I want you for all time, ___ And the Wi - chi - ta

line - man is still on the line. ___

Work Song

Words by Oscar Brown, Jr.
Music by Nat Adderley

'Cause I been con - vict - ed o' crime.
When he caught me rob - bin' his store.
Heard my wom - an scream,___ "Law - dy, no!"
Lawd, it sure is hot ___ in the sun.

Chorus:

Hol' it stead - y right there___ while I hit it. There! I reck-on that___

___ ought - a git it. Been work-in'___ an' work-in', But I still ___

___ got so terr - 'ble long to go. ___

With A Little Help From My Friends

Words and Music by John Lennon and Paul McCartney

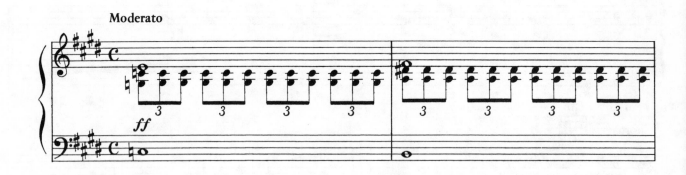

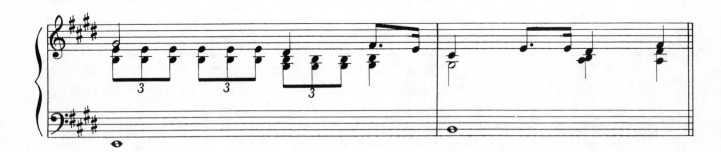

with a lit-tle help___ from my friends___   Mm,   I get high___

with a lit-tle help___ from my friends___

Mm I'm gon-na try___
Oh I'm gon-na try___

with a lit-tle help___ from my friends___

(Do you need___
(Do you need___

an-y-bod-y?) I need some-bod-y to love___
an-y-bod-y?) I just need some-one to love___

(Could it be___ an-y-bod-y?) I
(Could it be___ an-y-bod-y?) I

To Coda ⊕   *D.S. al Coda* 𝄋 Coda ⊕

want some-bod-y to love___
want some-bod-y to love___

___ Oh, I get by___

___ with a lit-tle help___ from my friends___ Mm, I'm gon-na try___

Yellow Submarine

Words and Music by John Lennon and Paul McCartney

274

Your Song

Words and Music by Elton John and Bernie Taupin

I don't_ have much mon - ey,_____ but   boy, if I   did._____
know_ it's not   much_ but it's the   best _ I can   do._____
But the sun's been quite kind, _____   while I wrote this   song,_____
An - y - way___ the   thing _____ is   what I real - ly   mean,_____

I'd buy_ a big house   where__   we both_ could live.
My gift_ is my song   and ___   keep it_ turned on.
It's for peo - ple like you,   that___   keep it_ turned on.
Yours are_ the_ sweet -est   eyes _____

this one's_ for you. ___
I've ev - er   seen. ___

And you__ can tell ev - 'ry - bod - y, This__ is your song._____

It may__ be quite__ sim - ple but, ___ now that it's done,_____

I hope you don't mind__ I hope you don't mind ____ that I put__ down in__ words, How

won - der - ful life is__ while you're__ in__ the world.__

Coda

I hope you don't mind,_ I hope you don't mind ___ that I put_down in words, How

Slower

won - der - ful life is ___ while you're ___ in_ the world. ___

1.

2.

you're_ in_ the world. ___

You're Sixteen

Words and Music by Bob Sherman and Dick Sherman

An Easy Four Feel

Ooh, you came out of a dream,— peach-es and cream,—

lips like straw-ber-ry wine._____ You're six - teen, __ you're

You're my ba-by, you're my pet, we fell in love on the

night we met. ___ You touched my hand, my heart ___ went 'pop,' ___ And

ooh, when we kissed we could not stop, ___ you walked out of my dreams, ___

Young Girl

Words and Music by Jerry Fuller

Moderately, with a rock beat

Young girl, get out of my mind,— my love for you is

way out of line.— Bet-ter run, girl, _____ you're much too young, girl. _____

1. With all the charms of a wom-an,
2. Be-neath your per - fume and make-up,
3. So hur-ry home to your ma - ma,

You've kept the se-cret of your youth.
You're just a ba-by in dis - guise.
I'm sure she won-ders where you are.

You led me to be-lieve_ you're old e-nough_ to
And though you know that it_ is wrong to be_ a-
Get out of here be-fore_ I have the time_ to

Index of Composers and Lyricists